MAR 0   1995

Jesse James and the Civil War in Missouri

Project Sponsors

Missouri Humanities Council and the National Endowment for the Humanities

Missouri State Library

Western Historical Manuscript Collection, University of Missouri–Columbia

Project Directors

Susanna Alexander

Rebecca B. Schroeder

Consultants

Virginia Lee Fisher

Charles T. Jones

Adolf E. Schroeder

Arvarh E. Strickland

Special Thanks

Patti Dudenhoeffer

Barbara Carroll Jones

Dealia Lipscomb

Adult Learning Center, Columbia

ABLE Learning Center, Jefferson City

Daniel Boone Regional Library, Columbia

Missouri Folklore Society

State Historical Society of Missouri, Columbia

Missouri Heritage Readers

General Editor, Rebecca B. Schroeder

Each Missouri Heritage Reader explores a particular aspect of the state's rich cultural heritage. Focusing on people, places, historical events, and the details of daily life, these books illustrate the ways in which people from all parts of the world contributed to the development of the state and the region. The books incorporate documentary and oral history, folklore, and informal literature in a way that makes these resources accessible to all Missourians.

Intended primarily for adult new readers, these books will also be invaluable to readers of all ages interested in the cultural and social history of Missouri.

Books in the Series

Food in Missouri: A Cultural Stew,
by Madeline Matson

Jesse James and the Civil War in Missouri,
by Robert L. Dyer

Jesse James
and the **Civil War**
in Missouri

ROBERT L. DYER

University of Missouri Press

COLUMBIA AND LONDON

Library of Congress Cataloging-in-Publication Data

Dyer, Robert, 1939-
   Jesse James and the Civil War in Missouri / Robert L. Dyer.
     p. cm. — (Missouri heritage readers)
   Includes bibliographical references (p.   ) and index.
   ISBN 0-8262-0959-9
   1. Missouri—History—Civil War, 1861–1865—Underground
movements. 2. James, Jesse, 1847–1882. 3. United States—
History—Civil War, 1861–1865—Underground movements.
4. Guerrillas—Missouri—Biography. 5. Outlaws—West
(U.S.)—Biography. 6. Frontier and pioneer life—West (U.S.)
I. Title. II. Series.
E470.45.D94 1994
364.1'552'092—dc20
[B]   93–50793
                                                                                 CIP

∞ This paper meets the requirements of the
American National Standard for Permanence of Paper
for Printed Library Materials, Z39.48, 1984.

Designer: Elizabeth K. Fett
Typesetter: Connell-Zeko Type & Graphics
Printer and binder: Thomson-Shore, Inc.
Typefaces: Goudy Old Style and Futura Bold

The publication of this book has been supported by a grant from

MISSOURI
HUMANITIES
COUNCIL

I thank my wife, Sharon, and my daughter, Amber, for the continual and unwavering support they give to my various creative projects as well as for their understanding of the long hours I often need to spend glued to my computer or rummaging in historical society collections.

Contents

Acknowledgments

I would like to express my special thanks to the other participants in this project who shared in the reading of this manuscript and in making suggestions to improve it.

I would also like to thank Dave Para and Cathy Barton for the part they played in leading me to the successful completion of this project. The three of us have worked together for the last six years or so in Missouri schools, presenting programs on Missouri history, art, folklore, and music through Young Audiences of Kansas City. It was the work we did on one of these projects, "The Brothers' War," about the Civil War in Missouri, Kansas, and Arkansas, that provided the seedbed for the flowering of this book. The three of us read and discussed a wide variety of books on the subject and also bounced a number of ideas off each other about the nature of Jesse James and other key actors in the "Border War" during the many months that went into the preparation of "The Brothers' War." This interaction contributed greatly to my understanding of the subject and led not only to the writing of this book, but also to our recording of a collection of Civil War songs from the Missouri area called *Johnny Whistletrigger*.

Thanks should also go to staff members of the State Historical Society of Missouri, especially Marie Concannon and Fae Sotham, for their help in locating source material and illustrations.

Jesse James and the Civil War in Missouri

Jesse James and Robin Hood

Jesse James is one of the most famous outlaws in American history. Many people think of him as an outlaw who stole from the rich and gave to the poor, a hero like Robin Hood. But was Jesse James really a "Robin Hood"?

The popular stories about Robin Hood are set in England in the thirteenth century. In the stories, Robin Hood does not like the way the poor people in England are treated by the king. Robin Hood and his "Merry Men" set poor people free when they are put in jail for hunting the king's deer. They also steal back money and property taken from the poor by the evil sheriff of Nottingham. The stories make Robin Hood a hero rather than a bad man, and many songs were made up about him.

What about Jesse James? Was he a hero? Or was he just a common thief and a cold-blooded killer? How did he become such a famous person?

> Livin' in Missouri was a bold bad man
> Known from Seattle down to Birmingham
> From Denver, Colorado, right across the state
> From Boston, Massachusetts to the Golden Gate.
> —*Vance Randolph*, Ozark Folksongs
> (*University of Missouri Press, 1980*), *vol. 2*

Jesse James was born in 1847 on a small farm near the town of Kearney, in Clay County, Missouri. He grew up during the

Jesse James (1847–1882). (State Historical Society of Missouri)

troubled years just before and during the American Civil War. When the Civil War began in 1861, Jesse was fourteen years old. He left home to fight in the war when he was sixteen years old. When the war ended in the spring of 1865, Jesse was seventeen years old. That was when he and his older brother,

Frank, along with some of the men who fought with them during the Civil War, became outlaws.

Between 1866 and 1882 the James gang robbed banks and trains in Missouri and several other states. Most of the banks and railroads were owned by people who had been on the Northern, or Union, side during the Civil War. The banks charged high interest rates on loans to people trying to rebuild their farms and businesses after the war was over. People were forced to pay taxes to support the railroads. Then the railroads charged high freight rates to farmers trying to ship livestock and crops to market after the war.

People living in Missouri were unhappy with the way they were treated by the banks, the government, and the railroads. Many of these people had been on the Southern, or Confederate, side during the war, so they were not very upset when the James gang robbed a bank or a train. Some people even helped the gang hide when they were being hunted by lawmen.

Because of the James gang, Missouri was called the "Robber State" or the "Outlaw State." Missouri's governor, Thomas T. Crittenden, a former Union officer, did not want the state to have a bad name, so in 1881 he offered a big reward for Jesse's capture. Finally, in 1882, Jesse was killed by one of his own men. Jesse was thirty-five years old when he was shot in the back of the head by Robert Ford in St. Joseph, Missouri. Not long after Jesse was killed, his brother Frank surrendered and the career of the James gang ended.

But this was not the end of the James legend. Soon after Jesse's death, songs were written about him. The songs spread all over America. Many different songs were sung, and many stories about Jesse James were told. Many magazine and newspaper articles, as well as books, have been written about Jesse James over the last hundred years. Movies and TV shows have been made about him.

People in rural areas of Missouri, Iowa, Kansas, Minnesota, Arkansas, Kentucky, and Tennessee still tell Jesse James sto-

The proclamation by Governor Thomas T. Crittenden offering a reward for the capture of Frank and Jesse James. (State Historical Society of Missouri)

ries handed down to them by their grandparents and great-grandparents. He has become an American folk hero. Because of this it is not easy to know what is true and what is not true in the stories about his life.

Even while Jesse was still alive it was hard to learn the truth about him. He and his gang were often blamed for robberies and killings they had nothing to do with. One well-known Missouri newspaper editor and writer, John Newman Edwards, wrote stories about Jesse James that made him seem like a hero. Edwards compared Jesse James to Robin Hood. Jesse and Frank James also compared themselves to Robin Hood and to Dick Turpin, a famous English outlaw of the early 1700s.

To understand the legend of Jesse James we need to look more closely at the American Civil War and especially at what happened in Missouri during the war.

How the Civil War Came to Missouri

Slavery was not the only cause of the Civil War, but it was one of the main causes. During the eighteenth century more than half a million Africans were brought to America and sold into slavery to work on big farms, called plantations, in the Southern states. One of the main crops grown on the plantations was cotton. The Southern states were sometimes called "The Cotton Kingdom." Other important plantation crops were tobacco, rice, and sugar.

Growing and harvesting plantation crops was hard work and took a large number of strong, cheap laborers. That is why plantation owners wanted slaves. The wealth and power of the Southern states were based on slave labor.

In the Northern states most of the wealth and power was based on manufacturing, or the making of things. Slave labor was not as important for manufacturing as it was for plantation farming, so slavery did not become a part of life in the Northern states. In fact, slavery was not allowed in the Northern states.

By 1819 political power in America was divided between an equal number of Southern slave-owning states, where plantation farming was the main way of life, and Northern states, where manufacturing was becoming more important than farming. When settlers formed new territories in the lands west of the Mississippi River, politicians on both sides saw a chance

$100 REWARD:

RAN AWAY from the subscriber, living in Boone county, Mo. on Friday the 13th June,

THREE NEGROES,

VIZ   DAVE, and JUDY his wife; and JOHN, their son. Dave is about 32 years of age, light color for a full blooded negro— is a good boot and shoe maker by trade : is also a good farm hand. He is about 5 feet 10 or 11 inches high, stout made, and quite an artful, sensible fellow. Had on when he went away, coat and pantaloons of brown woollen jeans, shirt of home made flax linen, and a pair of welted shoes. Judy is rather slender made, ab.ut 28 years old, has a very light complexion for a negro; had on a dress made of flax linen, striped with copperas and blue; is a first rate house servant and seam- stress, and a good spinner, and is very full of affectation when spoken to. John is 9 years old, very likely and well grown; is remark- ably light colored for a negro, and is cross- eyed. Had on a pair of brown jeans panta- loons, bleached flax linen shirt, and red flan- nel one under it, and a new straw hat.

I will give the above reward and all reas- onable expenses, if secured any where out of the State, so that I can get them again, or $50 if taken within the Staie—$30 for Dave alone, and $20 for Judy and John, and the same in proportion out of the state. The a- bova mentioned clothing was all they took with them from home, but it is supposed he had $30 or $40 in cash with him, so that he may buy and exchange their clothing.

WILLIAM LIENTZ.
Boone county, Mo. June 17, 1834:   52-2

A newspaper ad offering a reward for run- away slaves from Boone County. (State His- torical Society of Missouri)

to get more power. When these new territories started asking to
be admitted to the Union as states, the question of whether
they would be slave states or free states became important.

The first test came in 1819 when the Missouri Territory
asked to be admitted to the Union as a state. At that time
there were twenty-two states, eleven slave and eleven free.
Most of the people who settled the Missouri Territory came
from Southern states, and some of these people brought slaves
with them. They wanted Missouri admitted as a slave state.
But admitting Missouri as a slave state would upset the balance between slave and free states.

At the same time Missouri was asking to be admitted as a
state, the territory of Maine in the northeast also asked to be
admitted as a state. To solve the problem of balancing slave
and free states, Congress decided in 1821 to admit Maine as a
free state and Missouri as a slave state. Congress also decided
that from then on no other western territories north of a line
that ran along the southern border of Missouri would be
admitted as slave states. This ruling by Congress was known as
the Missouri Compromise. It solved the problem for a while.

The problem of balancing slave states and free states came
up again in the 1850s when the Kansas and Nebraska territories along the western borders of Missouri and Iowa asked to
be admitted to the Union. Both of these territories were north
of the line that had been set by the Missouri Compromise. If
they were both admitted as free states, then the balance between free and slave states would be upset. If one were admitted as a free state and the other as a slave state, there would be
a balance, but the Missouri Compromise would be violated.

Congress decided to repeal the Missouri Compromise in
the Kansas-Nebraska Act of 1854. The government said that
from then on the question of whether territories would be
admitted to the Union as free states or slave states would be
left to a vote of the people living in the territories.

Everyone knew Nebraska would vote to come into the
Union as a free state, but Kansas was another matter. Slave

owners in Missouri, especially those living near the border of
the Kansas Territory, did not want to see Kansas come into
the Union as a free state. Many of these Missourians began to
move into Kansas so they could vote for slavery in the upcom-
ing election.

Although many people in the free Northern states were
not against the idea of slaves being kept in the Southern
states, they were upset that the government had made it
possible for slavery to spread north of the Missouri Compromise line and into the Western territories. They thought this
would give the slave states too much political power. Some
people in the Northern states wanted to get rid of slavery
altogether. These people were called "Abolitionists." After
the Kansas-Nebraska Act of 1854 was passed, Northerners
who wanted to stop the spread of slavery and Abolitionists,
who wanted to get rid of slavery altogether, began moving
into Kansas to vote against slavery in the election.

At the first election in 1855 the people in favor of slavery
won. But the people who were against slavery said the election was unfair. As a result of this argument over the election,
two different state governments with two different constitu-
tions were set up in Kansas.

The arguments between the people who were for slavery
and the people who were against slavery became louder and
more violent. It wasn't long before fighting began. Between
1856 and 1860 pro-slavery and anti-slavery supporters fought a
bloody war along the Kansas and Missouri border for control
of the Kansas Territory.

The federal government finally said the free state government in Topeka, Kansas, would represent the state when it
was admitted to the Union in 1861. This decision made people in Missouri and the other slave states angry. But this was
only one of many decisions by the federal government during
this time that angered people in the slave states. More and
more of the slave states were saying it was time to leave the
United States of America and form their own nation.

In 1860 Abraham Lincoln was elected president of the United States. Lincoln represented the newly formed Republican Party. This political party was made up of people who were against the spread of slavery beyond the Southern states.

When Lincoln was elected, Southern states began leaving the Union. They formed the Confederate States of America and elected Jefferson Davis as president. He had been the United States senator from Mississippi before he was elected president of the Confederacy.

Davis ordered federal troops to get out of all the Southern states. When federal troops would not leave Fort Sumter, in the harbor at Charleston, South Carolina, Davis ordered Confederate troops to attack the fort. On April 12, 1861, the Confederates attacked Fort Sumter. This caused Lincoln to take action against the Confederacy and was the real beginning of the Civil War.

The Civil War lasted for four long years. Most of the major battles in the war took place in the Southern states east of the Mississippi River, but states that bordered on this area, like Missouri and Kentucky, also saw their share of fighting and suffering.

Before we look at how the Civil War was fought in Missouri, and what this had to do with Jesse and Frank James, we need to take a closer look at the Border War between Kansas and Missouri in the years before the Civil War. The Border War made a strong impression on the James boys and on many other young men from both Kansas and Missouri who later fought in the Civil War.

Blood on the Border

The parents of Jesse and Frank James came to Missouri from Kentucky in 1842. The father, Robert James, was a well-educated, soft-spoken Baptist minister. The mother, Zerelda, was a tall, strong woman who was not afraid to speak her mind.

Robert and Zerelda James owned a few slaves and bought a small farm near Kearney (then called Centerville) in Clay County. Clay County is a Missouri county that touches the Kansas border. Robert and Zerelda raised sheep and cattle. Frank, their first child, was born in 1843. Jesse, their second child, was born in 1847. Susan, their third child, was born in 1849.

Robert James went to California in 1850, along with many other Missourians, to seek his fortune in the Gold Rush. But soon after he got to California, he got sick and died. Zerelda then married a man named Benjamin Simms, but they separated a few months later. Shortly after that he died, and in 1855 Zerelda married a doctor named Reuben Samuel. She stayed with him for the rest of her life. The children liked Dr. Samuel, and he raised them as if they were his own.

In 1856, when the Border War between Kansas and Missouri began, Frank was thirteen and Jesse was nine. They grew up hearing their neighbors talking angrily about being raided by gangs of anti-slavery "Jayhawkers" and "Redlegs" from Kansas. These gangs of men would ride up to a pro-slavery farm,

11

beat and sometimes kill the owner, steal his livestock, take any slaves he had, and often burn his house and barns.

The name *Jayhawker* came from a kind of bird that killed another bird by "playing" with it as a cat plays with a mouse until it is dead. The most dangerous Jayhawker band was led by Jim Lane. He was also a U.S. senator and a powerful politician in Kansas.

The other name commonly used for the gangs from Kansas was *Redlegs*. This name came from the fact that some gang members, especially those who rode with a man named Jim Montgomery, wore red leggings over the tops of their boots.

But the most hated of all the anti-slavery gang leaders was a wild-eyed, Bible-quoting Abolitionist named John Brown. Stories were told about John Brown and his sons hacking pro-slavery farmers to death with swords.

Frank and Jesse James, along with other children of pro-slavery families, played a game called Old John Brown. Some-one would take the part of John Brown and someone else would be his victim. The other children would come to the rescue of the victim, and together they would drive John Brown back into Kansas, swearing to get revenge on him some day.

Some Missourians actually did form gangs to get revenge for the raids by the Jayhawkers and Redlegs. People in Kansas called these Missouri pro-slavery gangs "Border Ruffians." A *ruffian* is a rough and tough person. The anti-slavery people in Kansas used this word to give the pro-slavery people a bad name. One of these Border Ruffians was a strange young blue-eyed man named William Clarke Quantrill.

Quantrill came to Kansas from Ohio in 1857 as a school-teacher. At first he was on the side of the anti-slavery people in Kansas, but something caused him to change his mind. He told people later that he changed his mind after a group of anti-slavery men killed his brother and almost killed him. This story was not true, but at the time everyone believed it.

Quantrill changed sides in December 1860. He was with

Abolitionist John Brown (1800–1859) moved from Ohio to Kansas
in 1855. He believed he had been sent by God to destroy pro-slavery
settlers. (State Historical Society of Missouri)

William Clarke Quantrill (1837–1865) became a "bushwacker" and guerrilla. (State Historical Society of Missouri)

some anti-slavery men from Kansas who were planning a raid on a pro-slavery farm owned by Morgan Walker near Blue Springs, Missouri. Before the raid began, Quantrill went to the Walkers' farm and told them what was about to happen. He agreed to lead the anti-slavery men into a trap set by the

Walkers. One of the Kansans was killed, and another one was wounded when they were surprised by the Walkers.

From this time on Quantrill was a strong pro-slavery man. When the Civil War began in 1861 he became one of the main leaders of a gang of "bushwhackers" who fought on the Southern, or Confederate, side in Missouri. They were called "bushwhackers" because they lived in the "bush," or country, and their legs "whacked" the bushes as they rode.

The Jayhawkers in Kansas joined forces with the Union army during the Civil War and continued to fight the Missouri bushwhackers just as they had done before the war began. But for the first several months of the Civil War in Missouri, the main fighting was between Missouri State Militia troops (known as the State Guard) and Union army troops.

Opening Guns

Missouri's governor, Claiborne Fox Jackson, wanted Missouri to join the Southern states when those states began to leave the Union in early 1861. Other people in the Missouri government wanted to keep Missouri in the Union. A state convention was held in March 1861 to decide what to do. The people who attended the convention decided that Missouri should stay in the Union.

Governor Jackson did not agree with the decision of the convention. He began working on a secret plan to get control of the guns and ammunition stored at the U.S. Arsenal in St. Louis. He wanted to take control of those arms so the State Guard would have the power to help him take Missouri out of the Union. He ordered the State Guard to meet at a place in St. Louis called Camp Jackson. They planned to march on the arsenal and capture it.

Jackson's plan might have worked if Union Captain Nathaniel Lyon had not found out what was about to happen. Captain Lyon acted quickly. He surrounded the camp with several thousand of his men and forced the State Guard to surrender.

Then Lyon made the mistake of marching the captured State Guard troops through the streets of St. Louis. Crowds of angry people gathered and began shouting and throwing rocks at Lyon and his Union army troops. Shots were fired. Several

The U.S. Arsenal in St. Louis, where Governor Jackson hoped to get arms. (State Historical Society of Missouri)

soldiers and more than twenty people in the crowd were killed. Other people were injured.

Many of the Union troops were German, and they were blamed for what happened by pro-slavery Missourians, many from Southern states. Germans had been coming to Missouri in large numbers since the 1830s. Most of these immigrants settled along the Missouri River between St. Louis and Hermann, but others settled in central and western Missouri. Most of the Germans were against the idea of slavery and took the side of the federal government in the Civil War.

Angry newspaper articles were published about the so-called Camp Jackson Massacre, and songs were even written about it. One of these songs was called "The Invasion of Camp Jackson by the Hessians." The word *Hessians* was another word used for "Germans." Soldiers from Hesse in Ger-

U.S. volunteer troops were attacked on the corner of Fifth and Walnut streets in St. Louis on May 11, 1861, the day after the fall of Camp Jackson. (State Historical Society of Missouri)

many had been brought to America by the English to fight in the Revolutionary War. Many had stayed in America, but most of the German immigrants in Missouri were not from Hesse. The term just became a popular word for Germans. Germans are also sometimes referred to as the "Dutch," and both terms were used in Civil War songs. Here is a verse and a chorus from "The Invasion of Camp Jackson by the Hessians," which was sung to an old tune called "The Happy Land of Canaan." The word *Canaan* in the song comes from the Bible.

Our boys looked so neat, when they formed upon the street,
You could tell that saur kraut was not their feeding;
Our men were straight and tall, the Dutch were thin and small
And a disgrace to our happy land of Canaan.

CHORUS
Oh! oh! oh! ah! ah! ah! the time of our glory is coming.
We yet will see the time, when all of us will shine.
And drive the Hessians from our happy land of Canaan.
—*Composed by Joe Leddy and sung in Jefferson City*
in 1861

The Camp Jackson affair did more than anything else to make many Missourians decide to take Governor Jackson's side, join the State Guard, and try to force the Union army out of Missouri. General Sterling Price had been Missouri's governor during the Kansas-Nebraska dispute. He agreed to lead Jackson's State Guard, and it was not long before fighting began.

There was, however, one last attempt by both sides to find a way to keep the peace. Lyon and his main supporter in Missouri, Francis Blair, met with Governor Jackson and General Price at the Planter's House Hotel in St. Louis on June 11, 1861.

The meeting did not go well. Jackson said he would not give the order for any Missouri troops to join the Union army. He also told Lyon, who was now a general, to take his Union army troops out of the state. This demand angered Lyon. He told Jackson and Price that their words and actions left him no choice but to go to war against them.

Jackson and Price left the Planter's House and took a train to Jefferson City, burning railroad bridges behind them. Governor Jackson called for fifty thousand men to join him and drive the Union army out of the state. He said that anyone who wanted to join him should come to either Boonville or Lexington and sign up. Both towns were on the Missouri River, and both towns were known to have many strong Southern supporters. Jackson and Price then left for Boonville to help organize the men who were meeting there.

General Lyon and his Union army troops went after the State Guard. Lyon captured Jefferson City on June 14. Then he headed for Boonville with his well-trained and well-armed men.

The "fateful meeting" between General Nathaniel Lyon, Francis Blair, Governor Claiborne Fox Jackson, and General Sterling Price in the Planter's House, June 11, 1861. (State Historical Society of Missouri)

The Battle of Boonville, June 17, 1861. (State Historical Society of Missouri)

General Price had left Boonville to go to Lexington to help organize the volunteers there. One of those volunteers was eighteen-year-old Frank James. He had joined a local group of "Home Guards" at Centerville, not far from the James farm, a few weeks before Price came to Lexington. His brother Jesse also wanted to join, but he was only fourteen at the time. His mother thought he was too young to go, so she kept him at home.

Back at Boonville, Governor Jackson ordered his men to try to stop Lyon's men, who were now marching on Boonville. But the State Guard troops never really had a chance. Lyon's attack made the State Guard turn and run so fast that the battle was called "The Boonville Races."

The fighting at Boonville was an important win for the Union army. Jackson had to retreat south toward Arkansas, and Union troops took control of the Missouri River and the state government.

When Price heard about the defeat at Boonville, he also took his troops south and joined Jackson's troops in southern

Missouri. They were attacked at Carthage, Missouri, by Union troops under the command of General Franz Sigel, a St. Louis German. He had been sent to southern Missouri earlier by General Lyon with the idea of trying to stop Price and Jackson from joining Confederate troops in Arkansas.

General Sigel did not have nearly enough men to stop Jackson and Price, but he did slow them down at the Battle of Carthage. Sigel then retreated to Springfield to wait for Lyon to arrive with additional Union army troops. The scene was set for the biggest and most important battle fought in Missouri during the Civil War, the Battle of Wilson's Creek.

The Battle of Wilson's Creek

General Price and Governor Jackson continued to march south after fighting General Sigel at Carthage. They joined forces with the Confederate army from Arkansas under General Ben McCulloch. Price and McCulloch together had about twelve thousand men. They decided to attack the Union troops at Springfield. The troops under General Price and General Mc-Culloch began marching toward Springfield and camped for the night along Wilson's Creek just south of the town.

Generals Lyon and Sigel had only about six thousand Union troops, so Lyon sent a message to the Union army headquarters in St. Louis asking for help. When he found out he was not going to get any help, he decided he might be able to defeat Price and McCulloch by making a surprise attack during the early morning hours. At dawn on August 10, 1861, General Sigel attacked General McCulloch's men from the south and Lyon attacked Price's men from the north. At first things seemed to be going well for the Union army, but the Confederates under General McCulloch finally forced Sigel to retreat. Many soldiers were not in uniform, and Sigel's men had mistaken some of McCulloch's troops for Union troops.

General Price then ordered his State Guard troops to attack General Lyon's men on a high hill overlooking the valley of Wilson's Creek. So many people on both sides were killed during this part of the battle that the place was called "Bloody

General Franz Sigel, a German immigrant who was teaching in St. Louis when the Civil War broke out, fought at Wilson's Creek and Pea Ridge. (State Historical Society of Missouri)

General Lyon, shown on his white horse, was killed at the Battle of Wilson's Creek. (State Historical Society of Missouri)

Hill." Lyon's men were able to hold the hill, but Lyon was killed. He was the first Union general to be killed during the Civil War.

The death of Lyon and the large number of Union soldiers killed and wounded during the fighting at Bloody Hill made it necessary for the Union army to retreat to Springfield and then to St. Louis. The Confederate and State Guard armies also had many men killed and wounded, but the Battle of Wilson's Creek was a victory for the Confederate forces. Southern sympathizers made up many songs about Sigel and his "Dutch" troops who fought at Wilson's Creek.

> Old Sigel fought some on that day
> But lost his army in the fray.
> Then off to Springfield he did run
> With two Dutch guards and nary a gun.
> —*Randolph*, Ozark Folksongs, *vol. 2*

Wilson's Creek was the first major battle west of the Mississippi River. Among the men who fought on the Confederate side were Frank James, William Clarke Quantrill, and Cole Younger. Frank James, Jesse's older brother, had joined Price's army at Lexington. Quantrill had been a fierce fighter for the Missourians during the Kansas-Missouri Border War. Cole Younger was from a wealthy family that lived in Harrisonville, Missouri, just south of Kansas City. After the war he and his brothers would become well-known members of the Jesse James gang.

One story about what happened to Frank James after the Battle of Wilson's Creek says that he got the measles shortly after the battle and was left at a hotel in Springfield. Union troops captured him, but later let him go after he promised he would go back to his home and not fight again for the rest of the war. Frank did go back home to Clay County, but he did not keep his promise to stay out of the war.

The Battle of Lexington

After the victory at Wilson's Creek more men joined General Price's State Guard. He decided to follow up his victory by marching north and trying to win back the towns along the Missouri River. He thought if he was successful he would try to recapture Jefferson City, so he could put Jackson back in control of the state government.

The first important river town Price wanted to capture was Lexington. This town was defended by Colonel James A. Mulligan's Twenty-third Illinois Infantry, a small force of about twenty-five hundred men known as the Irish Brigade. Mulligan knew he was going to be attacked and tried to get the Union army command in St. Louis to send help. The help did not get there in time. Price attacked Mulligan's men and finally forced them to surrender, but not until the Irish Brigade had held Price's army off for more than a week.

This battle is sometimes called the "Battle of the Hemp Bales" because Price's men used bales of hemp as shields when they made the final attack on Mulligan's troops. Hemp was a plant used to make rope at the time of the Civil War.

Quantrill probably fought in the Battle of Lexington, but he was getting tired of taking orders. After the battle he left Price to form his own group of irregular soldiers, or guerrillas, that was to become famous along the Kansas-Missouri border. Soon Frank James, Cole Younger, and others joined Quantrill.

The "Battle of the Hemp Bales" in Lexington was fought in September 1861. (State Historical Society of Missouri)

Jesse James would also join the guerrillas before the war was over.

Although the Battle of Lexington was another victory for Price, he was not able to follow up on his success. The main body of Union troops in Missouri was marching toward Lexington to attack him, and he was running low on supplies. He needed to go south again to reorganize and get more supplies. He also wanted to have his State Guard troops become part of the regular Confederate army.

General Price's troops marched to Neosho in southwestern Missouri, where Governor Jackson called a meeting of the members of the Missouri State Legislature still loyal to him. They voted to take Missouri out of the Union and join the Confederate government. Now General Price and his State Guard troops were a regular part of the Confederate army, and they were in control of southern Missouri.

Back in the state capitol at Jefferson City, however, the part of the state legislature that remained loyal to the Union voted against Jackson. They said they no longer considered him to be the governor of the state. They appointed a new temporary governor named Hamilton Gamble. From this time on there were two Missouri governments—one that was part of the Confederacy and one that was part of the Union.

Jackson first went to Arkansas with his family and twenty slaves. The *True Democrat* of Little Rock, Arkansas, published an interview with him on July 25, 1861. In it he said, "You see before you a fugitive from my own state, pursued by Federal bayonets. With two hundred men we fought the Hessians as long as we could."

He later settled his family in Texas and worked to set up camps for Missourians who wanted to go south to join the Confederates. After Jackson's death in Arkansas in December 1862, Lieutenant Governor Thomas C. Reynolds took over the Missouri government in exile. He set up headquarters first in Arkansas and then in Marshall, Texas. This Missouri government was recognized by the Confederacy.

The Battle of Pea Ridge

When General Henry Halleck took command of Union troops west of the Mississippi River, he decided to drive Price out of southern Missouri. He ordered one of the main Union generals under his command, Samuel R. Curtis, to go after Price. Curtis was able to push Price into Arkansas. He also forced General Ben McCulloch's Arkansas and Louisiana Confederates to retreat from their winter camp near the Missouri-Arkansas border.

Price's five thousand men then joined with McCulloch's fifteen thousand men and with five thousand Native Americans, mostly from the Cherokee tribe, who were led by General Albert Pike. They met near a place called Pea Ridge in Arkansas, not far from the Missouri border. Confederate General Earl Van Dorn was placed in command of this combined army of twenty-five thousand men, and a plan was made to attack the fifteen thousand men under the command of General Curtis.

The battle began on March 7, 1862, and at first the Confederate forces were able to push the Union army back. But General McCulloch was killed on the first day of the battle, and General Pike's Cherokee troops decided not to fight any more after making one wild charge into Union lines. General Price's Missourians made a good show of strength against Union troops near a place called Elkhorn Tavern, but Confed-

The Battle of Pea Ridge in northwest Arkansas. (State Historical Society of Missouri)

erate troops suffered heavy losses during the first day's fighting. They were also running low on ammunition and supplies.

On the second day of fighting the Union army attacked the weakened Confederate army and drove it from the field. It took the Confederate army nearly two weeks to get reorganized after this battle, and General Price was no longer able to seriously consider driving the Union army out of Missouri.

Price had another problem. Although he and his men were now part of the regular Confederate army, they got few supplies and very little support from the Confederate government. Price also learned that his men would probably be ordered to help Confederate troops east of the Mississippi River.

When Price's men heard they might be taken away from the defense of their home state, many of them decided to go back to their homes so they could help protect their families and friends. Most of the returning soldiers soon joined the gangs of guerrillas, like the one formed by Quantrill, that were roaming around central and western Missouri at this time. The war in Missouri became a "guerrilla" war after the Confederate defeat at Pea Ridge.

Guerrilla War

The word *guerrilla* is a Spanish word that means a common, everyday citizen who fights to defend his home territory against an invading army. Guerrillas fight in small groups, usually led by someone with a strong personality. These guerrilla bands are not part of a regular army. They move from place to place making surprise attacks on their enemies. They get their guns, ammunition, and other supplies from the raids they make or from people living in the countryside who support their actions.

Most of the fighting in Missouri during 1862, 1863, and 1864 was between guerrillas and regular Union army troops, or between guerrillas and Jayhawkers from Kansas. Jayhawkers continued to make raids into Missouri throughout the war. Very few of the fights could actually be called battles, but the fighting was constant and often brutal.

William Clarke Quantrill led the largest and best-known band of guerrillas in Missouri. Anyone who wanted to join Quantrill's band was asked only one question: "Will you follow orders, be true to your comrades, and kill those who serve and support the Union?" Frank James and Cole Younger were two of the people who answered "yes" to this question and joined Quantrill.

When Frank James returned to the family farm near Kearney, Missouri, after the Battle of Wilson's Creek, he was arrested almost as soon as he got home. His mother was able to get him released, but only after he signed an agreement saying he would never again take up arms against the Union. Frank, of course, did not let this agreement keep him from running off to join Quantrill's guerrillas as soon as he was set free.

Another well-known guerrilla leader was William C. Anderson, known as "Bloody Bill" Anderson. He got the nickname "Bloody Bill" because of the many men he killed, and because he seemed to go almost crazy in battles. Stories are told that he rode into battles screaming and foaming at the mouth like a mad dog. He was a tall man with high cheekbones and long black hair. People who knew him always made a point of talking about his eyes. One man said he had eyes that were a cross between the eyes of an eagle and those of a snake.

Bill Anderson was in his mid-twenties when the Civil War began. He grew up in Huntsville, Missouri, but his family moved to Kansas in 1854. He probably took part in some of the Kansas Border War fighting, but not much is known about him during that time. When the Civil War started, he formed a band of guerrillas that sometimes operated on its own and sometimes rode with Quantrill's men.

Guerrilla bands, like those led by Quantrill and Anderson, roamed the Missouri and Kansas countryside making quick surprise attacks on Union troops; they killed people suspected of being Union army supporters, tore up railroad tracks, and stole supplies. Union army troops and Jayhawkers tried to stop the guerrillas, but their job was made harder because many people living in the towns and in the countryside helped the guerrillas whenever they could.

Union troops often arrested, beat, and even killed people they thought might be helping the guerrillas, but these kinds of actions just made the guerrillas angrier and more brutal. Bill Anderson's sister was arrested by Union troops and locked up in a building in Kansas City. The building collapsed, and she was killed. Some people say that is why Anderson became

Guerrilla William C. Anderson was called "Bloody Bill." (State Historical Society of Missouri)

such a brutal and crazed killer. Many of the men and young boys who rode with the guerrillas were there to get revenge for things Union soldiers had done to their families. Sometimes the guerrillas scalped the men they killed. Sometimes they cut off fingers or ears. They did not often take prisoners.

Quantrill's Raid on Lawrence and Order No. 11

> All routing and shouting and giving the yell,
> Like so many demons just raised up from Hell.
> The boys they were drunken on powder and wine
> They came to burn Lawrence just over the line.
> —From "Quantrill," a ballad collected in Kansas

In August 1863 Quantrill led one of the bloodiest guerrilla raids of the war against the town of Lawrence, Kansas. This town stood for everything the Missouri guerrillas hated most. It was the home of the brutal Jayhawker Jim Lane, and many other Jayhawkers used the town as their home base.

At dawn on August 21, 1863, Quantrill rode into Lawrence with about four hundred and fifty men. This was the largest group of guerrillas Quantrill ever had under his command during the war. Frank James was one of Quantrill's men on this raid, and so was Cole Younger. Some people think Jesse James might have been with the guerrillas by this time, but most people believe he didn't join them until several months later.

For four hours Quantrill's men rode through the streets killing, burning, and stealing. By the time they left, they had killed over a hundred and fifty men and burned much of the town. They had hoped to find Jim Lane and kill him, but he was able to hide from them.

After the raid, Jim Lane was so angry that he insisted

The guerrilla war in Missouri and nearby states. Map reprinted by permission from *Gray Ghosts of the Confederacy* by Richard S. Brownlee, copyright © 1958 by Louisiana State University Press.

General Thomas Ewing, the commander of the Union troops along the Kansas-Missouri border, issue a famous order known as "Order No. 11." This order was issued on August 25, 1863. It required everyone living in the countryside in the Missouri counties of Jackson, Cass, Bates, and parts of Vernon along the Kansas border to leave their homes by September 9. If they did not leave, they would be taken from their homes by force. The reason for this action was that many of the families

Order No. 11 was painted by George Caleb Bingham to show how western Missouri families were driven from their homes. (State Historical Society of Missouri)

of the guerrillas lived in these counties, and the guerrillas often used homes in these counties as their base of operations.

The way Order No. 11 was carried out caused a great deal of suffering to the people living along the border. Nearly every farmhouse and barn in the countryside was burned, people were beaten and killed, and many people's personal possessions were either destroyed or stolen.

Even supporters of the Union cause in Missouri were shocked by how the order was carried out. George Caleb Bingham, Missouri's great painter, was not only a Union supporter during the Civil War but also served as Missouri's state treasurer. He was so angry at Ewing that he later made a famous painting called *Order No. 11* just to show how much suffering the order caused.

By October 1863 Quantrill and his men were riding south toward Texas to spend the winter. On the way they attacked a column of Union cavalry and wagons near Baxter Springs, Kansas. The men in this column were part of Union General James G. Blunt's personal escort. Quantrill's men killed most of them.

Once in Texas, Quantrill found that he was beginning to lose control over his men. Some of them had not liked what had happened at Lawrence and at Baxter Springs. Others had just become unhappy with Quantrill as a leader. Some of the guerrillas, like Cole Younger, decided it was time to join the regular Confederate army. Others, like George Todd and "Bloody Bill" Anderson, formed their own guerrilla gangs and made plans to return to Missouri in the spring to fight the enemy in their own way. Frank James was part of "Bloody Bill's" gang, and he would soon be joined by his younger brother Jesse.

Jesse James Goes to War

Jesse James turned sixteen in the fall of 1863, and in the spring of 1864 he left home to join the guerrillas. He had been wanting to join his brother Frank and the other guerrillas for over a year, but his mother thought he was too young to go to war. She and her husband, Dr. Samuel, also needed help on the family farm. Then something happened that changed their minds.

One day a group of Union soldiers came riding up to the James farm looking for Frank. They tried to get Dr. Samuel to tell them where Frank was, but he wouldn't tell them anything. They tied his hands, put a rope around his neck, threw it over the limb of a tree, and pulled him up off the ground.

Then they saw young Jesse and went to get him. While they were trying to get Jesse to tell them where Frank was, Zerelda cut her husband down and took him in the house. He was still alive, but he was badly hurt. The soldiers beat Jesse, but he wouldn't tell them anything. Finally they left. After the soldiers were gone, Jesse told his mother he was going to join the guerrillas and get revenge on the Union soldiers for what they had done to him and to his stepfather.

Jesse James joined the guerrilla gang led by "Bloody Bill" Anderson in the spring of 1864 when the guerrillas began returning to Missouri from Texas, where they had spent the winter. Soon after Jesse joined Anderson's guerrillas he got a

Jesse James joined the guerrillas when he was sixteen. (Western History Collections, University of Oklahoma Library)

nickname that stuck with him for the rest of his life. The nickname was "Dingus." He got this nickname after he accidentally shot off the tip of the third finger on his left hand while he was cleaning his pistol. Jesse did not like to use curse words so he just shook his hand and said, "That's the doddingus pistol I ever saw." The other guerrillas thought this was so funny that from then on they called him "Dingus."

Jesse took part in several guerrilla raids during the summer and fall of 1864 and got wounded in one of those raids. In August 1864 he was with Bill Anderson at Rocheport, Missouri, on the Missouri River. Anderson's gang stayed in Rocheport for several days shooting at steamboats passing by and making life miserable for the people living in the town.

In September, Anderson and his men made an attack on Union troops guarding the town of Fayette, not far from Rocheport in central Missouri. The raid was poorly planned and was not successful. The Union troops used the town's brick courthouse as a fort, and several of Anderson's men were killed and wounded when they tried to attack the courthouse.

Only a few days after the attack on Fayette, Anderson and his men rode into Centralia, another central Missouri town. They stopped a train with twenty-three Union soldiers and other passengers on board. After robbing the regular passengers, Anderson told one of his men, Archie Clements, to "muster out" the soldiers. "Mustering out" a soldier means to let him out of the army. Archie Clements and several of the other guerrillas told the men to take off their uniforms and then began shooting them one by one.

After killing the soldiers, Anderson and his men set fire to the train and to the railroad station. Then they rode out of town, heading west. A company of Union soldiers rode into Centralia just after Anderson left. After seeing what Anderson's men had done, the Union soldiers went after Anderson. But Anderson saw them coming and set a trap for them. At least a hundred and thirty Union soldiers were killed.

Anderson's men now rode west toward Boonville. Anderson had gotten word that General Sterling Price was making a raid through Missouri, trying one last time to drive the Union army out of the state. But things were not going well for Price, and he sent word to the guerrillas to meet him at Boonville to talk over some plans he had for the guerrillas to help him.

Anderson met with Price and was given orders to ride into northern Missouri and tear up as much railroad track as he could on the line that ran across the state from Hannibal to St. Joseph. Not long after this, however, Anderson was killed when he and his men were ambushed in southern Ray County. Jesse James was with Anderson when the ambush took place, but he escaped. Price left Boonville and marched west toward Kansas City, where the last major battle of the Civil War in Missouri was fought.

The Last Great Rebel Raid in Missouri

General Price he made a raid, made a raid, made a raid
General Price he made a raid
An' lost many a soldier . . .
*—A game song, collected by a WPA worker in
Doniphan, Missouri*

General Price's final raid through the state of Missouri began in the fall of 1864 when he marched out of Arkansas with about twelve thousand men. His plan was to attack St. Louis, but along the way he decided to take a small Union army fort known as Fort Davidson near Pilot Knob, Missouri.

The attack on Fort Davidson did not go well. The fort was defended by a small force of Union soldiers under General Thomas Ewing. But there was a deep ditch all around the fort, and nearly fifteen hundred of Price's men were killed as they tried to attack. Price then decided to wait until dark; he planned to put his artillery into position on a high hill over-looking the fort and attack from both the front and the rear the next morning.

Ewing knew he could not continue to hold the fort, so he slipped his men out in the middle of the night and returned to St. Louis. Because Price lost so much time and so many men trying to capture Fort Davidson, he had to change his plans about attacking St. Louis.

He decided to march west toward the state capital, Jeffer-

The Battle of Pilot Knob was a serious blow to General Price's dream of gaining control of Missouri. (State Historical Society of Missouri)

son City, with the idea that he might be able to take over the seat of government in the state. But when he got to Jefferson City he found the city was heavily fortified. He also learned that a large Union force was coming after him from St. Louis.

Price kept moving west and made his next stop at Boonville on the Missouri River. There he met with "Bloody Bill" Anderson's guerrillas and gave them the orders to attack the railroad lines in northern Missouri. Price then continued marching west up the river toward Lexington, Independence, and Kansas City.

He had started from Arkansas with nearly twelve thousand men, but he now had only about nine thousand left. Ahead of him at Kansas City was General Curtis with twelve thousand Union troops. Behind him was Union General Alfred Pleasonton with nearly five thousand troops. Pleasonton had been chasing Price ever since his army left Jefferson City.

General Sterling Price was known as "Pap" Price to his troops.
(State Historical Society of Missouri)

As Price approached Kansas City he pushed across the Little Blue River, and by the evening of October 22 he had reached the hills and prairies just south of Brush Creek near the town of Westport. The next day Price sent part of his men south toward Fort Scott with the supply wagons so they would not be trapped and destroyed. He then ordered part of his remaining army to guard a crossing of the Big Blue River called Byram's Ford. They were supposed to keep Pleasonton's men from crossing the river at this point and attacking Price's rear.

The main part of Price's army then attacked General Curtis, and a fierce battle took place. At first the Confederates had some success, but then the greater numbers of the Union army troops began to turn the battle against the Confederates. The men trying to keep Pleasonton's army from crossing the Big Blue River at Byram's Ford held the crossing for a while, but Pleasonton finally overpowered them.

Price realized he was in great danger of having his whole army destroyed, so he ordered a retreat. His men started moving south along the Kansas-Missouri border. The Battle of Westport was over. Nearly a thousand men were killed, wounded, or captured on both sides during the battle, and Price's last effort to drive the Union army out of Missouri had come to a bloody end.

The War Ends and the
James Gang Is Born

With Price's defeat at Westport in the fall of 1864, the war in Missouri was nearly over. Curtis chased Price south along the Kansas border, driving what was left of his ragged army down into Texas.

Two of the main guerrilla leaders had been killed about the same time as the Westport battle. George Todd was killed by a Union sharpshooter just outside Independence a few days before the battle; and "Bloody Bill" Anderson was killed in a charge on Union troops in Ray County a few days after the battle. Jesse James and the other men who had been riding with Anderson went south to Texas after Anderson was killed.

Quantrill had been in hiding for several months before the Battle of Westport. When he heard about Price's defeat he gathered some of his most trusted men together, including Frank James, and left Missouri for Kentucky. Some of his men later said he had a plan to go to Washington, D.C., and assassinate President Abraham Lincoln.

But an actor named John Wilkes Booth had the same plan and killed Lincoln on April 15, 1865. Less than a week before the assassination, the Civil War came to an end when the main part of the Confederate army under General Robert E. Lee surrendered to Ulysses S. Grant at Appomattox Courthouse in Virginia on April 9.

Guerrilla leader Bill Anderson was shot to death near Richmond a month after the Centralia massacre. (State Historical Society of Missouri)

About a month after the end of the war, Quantrill and his men were surprised by some Union guerrillas in Spencer County, Kentucky, and Quantrill was shot in the back and taken prisoner. He died twenty-seven days later at the age of twenty-seven.

With the end of the war and the death of the main guerrilla leaders, many of the guerrillas were uncertain what to do. Since they were not part of the regular Confederate army, the normal rules of war did not apply to them. Men who had been part of the regular Confederate army were allowed to return to their homes in peace with no further threat of punishment. But guerrillas were looked upon as outlaws.

The federal government said it would not take any action against them as long as they surrendered and agreed to obey the laws of the land. But the state of Missouri said the guerrillas might be subject to arrest and prosecution as outlaws. Many of the guerrillas did surrender, and most of them were allowed to return to their homes in peace. But several of the guerrillas, including Frank and Jesse James, did not surrender.

Some people say that Jesse James actually did try to surrender in May or June 1865, but he was shot and badly wounded by a Union soldier as he rode toward Lexington to give himself up. He managed to escape and made it to Nebraska, where his parents were living after being driven out of their home near Kearney as a result of Order No. 11.

His mother tried to nurse Jesse back to health, but he did not seem to improve very fast. He told his mother he wanted to go back home to Missouri. She took him as far as Kansas City, where they stopped at the home of his uncle John Mimms. Here, his cousin Zerelda, known as Zee, took over the job of nursing Jesse back to health. It was during this time that Jesse fell in love with his cousin Zee. They were to be married later.

While Jesse was recovering, his mother and stepfather returned to their home in Missouri and his brother Frank came

home from Kentucky. The two former guerrillas began making plans to form an outlaw gang. They were joined by several
other former guerrillas, including the Younger brothers. Over
the winter of 1865–1866 they planned their first robbery—of
the Clay County Savings Bank in Liberty, Missouri.

The First Bank Robberies (1866-1872)

On the afternoon of February 13, 1866, about a dozen men rode into Liberty, Missouri, and made their way to the Clay County Savings Bank. Two of the men went into the bank, pulled their pistols, and demanded money. When they left they had over $60,000. As the men rode out of town, one member of the gang thought he saw a young man trying to raise an alarm, so he shot and killed him. The whole gang then began firing wildly into the air and rode out of town toward the Missouri River.

This robbery is thought to be the first daylight robbery of a bank in peacetime in the history of the United States, and it was probably staged by the James gang. The young man killed in the robbery was a student at William Jewell College in Liberty named George Wymore.

Over the next year several more banks in Missouri and one in Kentucky were robbed by the gang that robbed the bank in Liberty. No one knows for sure if the James gang was responsible for all these robberies. But no one has much doubt that the James brothers robbed the Daviess County Savings Bank in Gallatin, Missouri, on December 7, 1869.

During this robbery the cashier, Captain John W. Sheets, was shot and killed by one of the men. The story goes that Jesse James killed Sheets because he thought he recognized him as the man who had killed "Bloody Bill" Anderson just

The Clay County Savings Bank in Liberty, Missouri, now a museum, was the first bank robbed by the James gang.

before the end of the war. Actually, the man responsible for killing Anderson was Major S. P. Cox, who also lived in Gallatin. Unfortunately, Captain Sheets looked a little like Cox.

There was so much bad feeling about the Gallatin robbery and killing that the James gang tried no more robberies for about a year. Then, on June 3, 1871, they robbed the bank at Corydon, Iowa, of $6,000; and in the spring of 1872 they robbed a bank in Columbia, Kentucky.

In the fall of 1872 they made one of their most daring robberies when they held up the cashier at the Kansas City fairgrounds in the midst of several thousand fairgoers. Just after this robbery the well-known newspaper writer John Newman Edwards wrote his first major article making the robbers sound almost like heroes. He did not say in his article that the robbers were Frank and Jesse James, but he described the men as former guerrillas and he praised them for their daring and their bravery. Here is part of what Edwards said in his newspaper article:

John Newman Edwards (1839–1889) wrote many news stories and a book about the guerrillas and Jesse James. (State Historical Society of Missouri)

These men are . . . bad because they live out of their time. . . . What they did we condemn. But the way they did it we cannot help admiring. . . . It was as though these bandits had come to us . . . with the halo of medieval chivalry upon their garments and shown us how the things were done that poets sing of.

Edwards had ridden with the great Missouri Confederate cavalry leader General Jo Shelby during the Civil War, and he was a strong supporter of the Southern point of view in his newspaper writing. He continued to write articles defending the James gang for many years. His writing did more to create the "legend" of Jesse James than almost anything else.

Edwards wrote most of the stories about Jesse James robbing from the rich and giving to the poor. He also printed letters in his newspaper, supposedly written by Jesse James, saying the James gang killed people only in self-defense and only robbed from rich people. Jesse would also often say that he and his gang were not the ones who had robbed a bank they were accused of robbing.

Trains and Pinkerton Men (1873–1876)

Less than a year after the Kansas City fairgrounds robbery, the James boys robbed their first train. They were not the first outlaws to rob trains. The Reno gang in Indiana was supposedly the first gang to rob a train. But Jesse and his gang became the most famous train robbers.

On July 21, 1873, Jesse and several members of his gang pulled a rail loose on the tracks of the Chicago, Rock Island and Pacific Railroad near Council Bluffs, Iowa. When the train came along, the engine was thrown off the track, killing the engineer. The gang members thought there was a big gold shipment on the train, but they were mistaken. They got only about $2,000 from the train safe along with some money and valuables from the passengers.

About six months after the Iowa train robbery, Jesse and his gang got several thousand dollars in a train robbery at Gads Hill, a small town in southeastern Missouri. During this robbery Jesse supposedly looked at the hands of the men on the train he was robbing to see which were working men. It is said that he did not rob those men, and he did not rob any of the women. He supposedly only robbed men who looked like they were rich.

About a month before the Gads Hill train robbery, John Newman Edwards wrote another long newspaper article about Jesse James and his gang. In this article Edwards told the

The Gads Hill train robbery by the James gang. (State Historical Society of Missouri)

whole story about why Jesse James had joined the guerrillas and how Jesse had almost been killed when he tried to surrender at the end of the war. Many of the stories in this article became important parts of the Jesse James legend. This article also has an interesting description of both Frank and Jesse James. Here is part of that description:

> Jesse James, the youngest, has a face as smooth and innocent as the face of a school girl. The blue eyes, very clear and penetrating, are never at rest. His form is tall, graceful and capable of great endurance and great effort. There is always a smile on his lips, and a graceful word or a compliment for all with whom he comes in contact. Looking at his small white hands, with their long tapering fingers, one would not imagine that with a revolver they were among the quickest and deadliest hands in all the west.
>
> Frank is older and taller. Jesse's face is a perfect oval—Frank's is long, wide about the forehead, square and massive about the jaws and chin, and set always in a look of fixed repose. Jesse is light-hearted, reckless, devil-may-care. . . . Neither will be taken alive.

The James gang was now being chased by the Pinkerton Detective Agency. Allen Pinkerton, the head of this agency, had been a Union spy during the Civil War. He put together his detective agency at the end of the war. When the James gang began robbing trains, the train companies hired the detectives to track down Jesse and his men.

The first three Pinkerton men who tracked the gang back to their home territory after the Gads Hill train robbery were killed—one not far from Kearney, and the other two near Monegaw Springs in St. Clair County. It was thought that Jesse and Frank killed the first man. The other two men were killed by the Younger brothers, but not before one of the Younger brothers himself was killed.

The robberies by the James gang and other outlaws, as well as the killing of the Pinkerton men, gave Missouri the reputation of being the "Outlaw State." The governor of Missouri at this time, Silas Woodson, tried to get a law passed that would give him money to hire detectives who could find and catch the outlaws, but he was not successful.

> Jesse James, Jesse James
> He robbed banks, and he robbed trains
> And the Pinkerton men tried to hunt him down;
> They followed him around from town to town
> But they never laid a hand on Jesse James.
> —Robert L. Dyer, *Big Canoe Songbook: Ballads from the Heartland* (Pekitanoui Publications, 1991)

All this publicity made the James gang even more famous. Many ordinary people in the state read the newspaper articles about the gang with great interest. Some citizens thought of Jesse and his men as their heroes. Jesse was their special favorite, and he became even more of a favorite after the newspapers announced he had secretly married his cousin Zee Mimms on April 23, 1874. Not long after Jesse and Zee were married, Frank married a woman from Jackson County named Annie Ralston.

In late August 1874, Jesse and Frank robbed a couple of stagecoaches near Lexington. They were also accused of robbing a bank in Mississippi and a train near Kansas City in December 1874. Zerelda Samuel did her best to convince witnesses and the newspapers that her sons were innocent of the robberies.

In late January 1875 the Pinkerton men staged a raid on the Samuels' farm near Kearney, but the raid backfired. Jesse and Frank had left the farm before the Pinkerton men arrived. The detectives thought they were still there and threw a bomb through one of the windows in the house. When the bomb exploded it killed Frank and Jesse's little half-brother, Archie Samuel. It also seriously injured their mother's right hand, and she later had to have her arm amputated above her elbow.

When the story about the Pinkerton raid appeared in newspapers many people were shocked. There was a movement in the state legislature to grant a special pardon to Jesse and Frank for the part they played in the Civil War and to grant them the right to a fair trial for the crimes they had been accused of since the end of the war. A bill was actually put before the state legislature on this matter, but it did not pass.

The James gang was accused of several robberies in Missouri and nearby states during 1875, and it was suspected of robbing a Missouri Pacific train near Otterville, Missouri, in July 1876. It is known for certain that the James gang tried to rob a bank in Northfield, Minnesota, in September 1876. This attempted robbery was nearly the end of the James gang.

Jesse and Frank James, along with Cole, Bob, and Jim Younger and three other men rode into Northfield on September 7. Three of the eight men walked into the First National Bank, drew their pistols, and told the cashier, Joseph L. Heywood, to open the safe. When he refused to open the safe they killed him. Another man working at the bank tried to escape and was wounded.

Townspeople heard the shooting, and several men armed themselves and went to the bank. A gun battle broke out on the streets of Northfield. Two of the outlaws were killed, and one was wounded. The rest of the gang galloped out of town.

The townspeople went after the outlaws. Several days later they caught up with four of them. They killed one and wounded the other three. The three wounded men—Cole, Bob, and Jim Younger—were captured. Jesse and Frank James escaped. Later, the Younger brothers were tried, found guilty, and sentenced to life in prison.

The Final Years (1877-1882)

After the disaster at Northfield, Minnesota, most of the gang members were either dead or in jail. Jesse and Frank decided to stay out-of-sight for a while, and they left Missouri. No one is sure where they lived for the next three years, but they were probably living in Tennessee.

What they did during this time is not clear. They may have been involved in trading cattle. Some writers who have studied the lives of Jesse and Frank James think the brothers were trying to get out of the outlaw business.

But on the night of October 8, 1879, a gang led by Jesse James robbed a Chicago and Alton Railroad train at the Glendale station, near Kansas City. Frank James was not involved with this robbery. He had probably given up the outlaw life altogether by this time.

A few months after the Glendale train robbery a story went around that Jesse James had been killed, but the story was not true. Some people think the story may have been made up so that detectives would stop looking for Jesse.

By the summer of 1881 Jesse and his family had moved back to Missouri and were living in Kansas City, where Jesse was using the name J. T. Jackson. In the fall of 1881 they moved to St. Joseph, and Jesse took the name Thomas Howard. During this time Jesse may have been involved in a train robbery near

Winston, Missouri, and another one at a place called Blue Cut near Otterville, Missouri.

One interesting story about Jesse James during this time comes from Callaway County, Missouri. Some people in the county believe Jesse lived there for a few months under the name of Johnson, while he was hiding from the law officers trying to find him. He supposedly came to the old Unity Baptist Church southwest of Fulton one day saying he was a traveling singing teacher. The minister of the church put him in charge of the children's Sunday school singing sessions, and he was very popular with the children.

But shortly after Jesse began teaching singing as "Brother Johnson" people began asking questions about who he was and where he came from. The prosecuting attorney of Callaway County decided there was a good chance that "Brother Johnson" was, in fact, the outlaw Jesse James and decided to have him arrested. Someone who liked Jesse heard about the plan and told "Brother Johnson." On the day the sheriff and his deputies came to get "Brother Johnson" they found he had vanished. He was never seen in Callaway County again.

No one knows whether or not the story about Jesse in Callaway County is true, but it is true that time was running out for Jesse James. The newly elected governor of Missouri, Thomas T. Crittenden, was determined to rid the state of out-laws. He put up a reward of $5,000 each for the capture of Jesse and Frank James. He hoped this would cause one of the gang members to turn traitor. And that is exactly what happened.

One of the newer members of Jesse's gang was a man named Charles Ford. He had a younger brother named Robert, who also claimed he wanted to be part of the gang. Both Charles and Robert Ford had been staying with Jesse and his family in St. Joseph planning another robbery. What Jesse didn't know, however, was that Robert Ford had been in touch with Missouri Governor Thomas Crittenden. He was planning to collect the reward money by killing Jesse.

On the morning of April 3, 1882, Charles and Robert Ford

Jesse James was shot in his home in St. Joseph by Robert Ford, April 3, 1882. (State Historical Society of Missouri)

A crowd gathers around Jesse's home in St. Joseph after his death.
(Robert L. Dyer collection)

were with Jesse in the living room of his house in St. Joseph.
Jesse had just taken off his guns. He noticed that a picture on
the wall wasn't hanging straight and stepped up on a chair to
straighten it. Robert Ford then drew his pistol and shot Jesse
in the back of the head, killing him instantly.

The news was in all the papers. Some newspaper writers
doubted that the person killed really was Jesse James. After
all, stories had been spread before that he was dead, and the
stories had turned out to be untrue. But this time the story
was true. Jesse James was dead.

John Newman Edwards, the newspaper writer who had
written so many stories defending Jesse and his gang, called
Jesse's killer a low, mean coward. Edwards was also very critical
of Governor Crittenden for plotting Jesse's death with a person like Robert Ford.

Even people who did not like Jesse James were upset about
the way Jesse was killed. Newspapers all over the United

States carried stories about Jesse's life and death. He was well on the way to becoming a legend.

In the fall of 1882, Frank James surrendered to Governor Crittenden after a deal was worked out by John Newman Edwards to make sure Frank would get a fair trial. Over the next three years Frank James stood trial in several places for various crimes connected with the James gang. He was not convicted in any of these trials, and finally all charges against him were dropped. He lived the rest of his life quietly and died in 1915.

John Newman Edwards and others tried to get the Younger brothers released from the Minnesota prison where they had been put after the Northfield raid. Edwards died in 1889 not long after preparing an unsuccessful petition for their release. A few months after Edwards's death, Bob Younger died in prison. Another attempt to free the remaining two Younger brothers failed in 1902. Soon after this failure, Jim Younger took his own life. Cole Younger was finally released from prison in 1903 and lived out the rest of his life in Lee's Summit, Missouri. He died in 1916.

The Legend of Jesse James

Jesse James was well on his way to becoming a legend before he was killed. After he was killed he became even more famous. Part of the reason for his fame was related to the emotions stirred up by the American Civil War. The James brothers and the Younger brothers fought on the Southern side as guerrillas during the Civil War. Since many other Missourians also supported the Southern cause during the war, they saw the James gang as a way of getting revenge on those who had supported the Northern side in the war.

Another reason for his fame was the angry feeling many people had toward the banks and railroads the James gang robbed. People felt that banks and railroads were taking advantage of them by charging high interest rates and high fees for freight. People in Missouri also believed most banks and railroads were owned by people who had supported the Northern cause in the Civil War.

The writings of John Newman Edwards also played an important part in creating the Jesse James legend. Edwards made a romantic hero out of Jesse James by comparing him to Robin Hood and to the Knights of the Round Table. Edwards also printed many of the popular stories that became such a big part of the Jesse James legend.

Soon after Jesse was killed a song about him was written, and this and other songs became popular all over the United

NOTED GUERRILLAS,

OR THE

WARFARE OF THE BORDER.

BEING A HISTORY OF THE LIVES AND ADVENTURES OF

QUANTRELL, BILL ANDERSON, GEORGE TODD, DAVE POOLE,
FLETCHER TAYLOR, PEYTON LONG, OLL SHEPHERD,
ARCH CLEMENTS, JOHN MAUPIN, TUCK AND
WOOT HILL, WM. GREGG, THOMAS MAU-
PIN, THE JAMES BROTHERS, THE
YOUNGER BROTHERS,
ARTHUR McCOY,

AND NUMEROUS OTHER WELL KNOWN

GUERRILLAS OF THE WEST.

BY

JOHN N. EDWARDS,

Author of "Shelby and His Men," "Shelby's Expedition to Mexico," Etc.

ILLUSTRATED.

John Newman Edwards's book on the guerrillas helped to create their legend: "They had passwords . . . and signals which meant everything or nothing. . . . They could see in the night like other beasts of prey and hunted most when it was darkest." (Robert L. Dyer collection)

States. Some songs say Jesse took from the rich and gave to the poor. Some list the banks and trains he robbed. Most tell about the way he was killed. One song says it was written by "Billy Gashade," but no one knows if there really was a person named Billy Gashade. Here are two verses and the chorus from one of the best-known versions of the song, the one "made by Billy Gashade."

> Jesse James was a lad that killed many a man.
> He robbed the Danville train.
> But that dirty little coward that shot Mr. Howard
> Has laid poor Jesse in the grave.
>
> It was Robert Ford, that dirty little coward,
> I wonder how he does feel;
> For he ate of Jesse's bread and slept in Jesse's bed
> And laid poor Jesse in the grave.
>
> CHORUS
> Poor Jesse had a wife to mourn for his life,
> His children they were brave;
> But that dirty little coward that shot Mr. Howard
> And laid poor Jesse in the grave!
> —H. M. *Belden*, Ballads and Songs Collected
> by the Missouri Folk-Lore Society (*University of Missouri Press, 1973*)

Mr. Howard, you will remember, is the false name Jesse lived under in St. Joseph, just before he was shot.

Plays about Jesse James and his gang began to appear in small-town opera houses throughout the Midwest only a few weeks after his death. One popular play that toured all over the country was called *The James Boys in Missouri*. Another play was called *Jesse James, the Bandit King*.

Popular magazines like the *Police Gazette*, the *New York Detective Library*, the *Five Cent Wide Awake Library*, the *Log Cabin Library*, and the *American Weekly* published sensational stories about Jesse James and his gang. The James gang was also the subject of many popular novels and several histories.

One of the earliest biographies of Jesse James was called *The Life, Times and Treacherous Death of Jesse James*. It was written by Frank Triplett, who claimed that much of the information in the book came directly from Jesse's widow, Zee James, and his mother, Zerelda Samuel. This book appeared within a month of Jesse's death.

The first attempt at a factual study of Jesse's life was a book by Robertus Love called *The Rise and Fall of Jesse James* published in 1926. Parts of this book appeared in St. Louis and Kansas City newspapers before being published in book form. Much of the information in this book is not based on fact, however.

In 1949 the well-known Missouri writer Homer Croy wrote a popular book about Jesse James called *Jesse James Was My Neighbor*. Croy was from Maryville, which is not too far from the James farm at Kearney. He grew up hearing stories about the James family from people who had known them.

Most of the books about Jesse James were written by people who seem to have admired him. These books are not always reliable as history. The one book that is most reliable as history is called *Jesse James Was His Name*. It was written by William A. Settle, Jr., a professor of American history at the University of Tulsa in Oklahoma, and was published by the University of Missouri Press in 1966.

Many movies and TV shows have also been made about Jesse James. Most of these are very unreliable as history, but they are often entertaining, and they keep the Jesse James legend alive. One of the most popular early movies was called simply *Jesse James*. It was made in 1939 and starred Tyrone Power as Jesse James and Henry Fonda as Frank James.

In 1957 Robert Wagner starred in another popular movie about Jesse James called *The True Story of Jesse James*. More recently there was a film called *The Long Riders* made in 1980, starring several sets of actor brothers in the parts of the James brothers, the Younger brothers, and the Ford brothers.

Books and made-for-TV movies continue to appear about

The James farm near Kearney. (Robert L. Dyer photo)

the James gang nearly every year. One of the most recent books, *I, Jesse James*, was written by James R. Ross, a great-grandson of Jesse James who is a Superior Court judge in Orange County, California.

The farm where Jesse and Frank were raised near Kearney, Missouri, is now a popular tourist attraction. The original farmhouse where Jesse was born and raised still stands, and a Jesse James museum has been built nearby. Every summer a play about Jesse James is put on at the James farm. The house in St. Joseph where Jesse James was killed is also a popular tourist attraction, as are banks robbed by Jesse James, like those in Liberty, Missouri, and Northfield, Minnesota.

The legend of Jesse James will probably be with us for a long time. People trying to find out the truth about his life still find new information that helps us understand him better. In early 1991 a Jesse James researcher named Ted Yeatman found an interesting letter among the papers of the Pinkerton

Detective Agency. The letter was written by Allen Pinkerton to a lawyer working for him in Liberty, Missouri, named Samuel Hardwicke. In the letter Pinkerton tells Hardwicke that when the men go to the James home to look for Jesse they should find some way to "burn the house down." He suggests that they use some kind of firebomb.

You may remember that when the Pinkertons made the raid on the James farm they threw something into the house that exploded. It blew off one of Jesse's mother's arms and killed his young half-brother. The Pinkertons always claimed this was an accident. They said they threw a flare into the house so they could see better, and that when Jesse's mother kicked it into the fireplace it exploded. But the letter found by Ted Yeatman seems to show that they deliberately threw a bomb of some kind into the house in an attempt to destroy it.

The Civil War as Living History

The Civil War continues to be of interest. People still have strong feelings about the war and about those who fought in it. From 1986 to 1990 there were many reenactments of Civil War battles in Missouri to mark the 125th anniversary of these battles. Several TV specials about the Civil War were shown during this same period, including one very popular series on PBS made by Ken Burns. A popular movie called *Glory*, about black soldiers in the Civil War, was released in 1991; another movie about the war, *Gettysburg*, was released in 1993.

In October 1992 an organization called the Sons of Confederate Veterans of the Civil War held a special ceremony at the old Confederate cemetery in Higginsville, Missouri. They buried five bones and a lock of hair believed to be some of the last remains of William Clarke Quantrill. These bones and the lock of hair had been found in the collection of the Kansas Historical Society. They were given to that society many years ago by a man who had gotten them when Quantrill's remains were moved from Kentucky, where he was killed, to Dover, Ohio, where he was born.

How the man got the bones and the lock of hair is not entirely clear. Some people were not even sure they were Quantrill's remains. Other people thought they should be returned to Dover, Ohio, to be buried along with his skull,

A Civil War reenactment group in Boonville. (Robert L. Dyer photo)

Descendants of members of Quantrill's guerrillas gather in Higgins-ville for the burial of his remains. (Elsa Hasch photo, *Columbia Daily Tribune*)

A monument to the "Blue and Gray" on the Pea Ridge Battlefield in Arkansas. (Robert L. Dyer photo)

which had been used for a number of years in a fraternity initiation ceremony until it was returned to Dover. But people in Dover, Ohio, were not too interested in drawing attention to the fact that Quantrill was born there.

Some people thought it was not right to bury Quantrill's remains at Higginsville because he supposedly was never commissioned as a regular officer in the Confederate army. Other people dispute this and say he was a commissioned Confederate officer. Some people objected to a ceremony honoring a man they believed was nothing more than a common outlaw and killer. Others believed he had fought as best he could for the South.

Despite all this controversy, the Sons of Confederate Veterans thought it was time to give Quantrill a proper burial and to recognize him for his service to the Confederate cause during the Civil War. The ceremony did, in fact, take place, and many people came to honor Quantrill's memory or because they were curious.

Newspapers all over the country, as well as TV news programs, reported on the ceremony, and strong comments both pro and con were made about the event. It is obvious that Quantrill is still a highly controversial subject to many people.

Less than a year before this ceremony took place a new book, called *Bloody Dawn,* about Quantrill and his raid on Lawrence, Kansas, came out. Thomas Goodrich, the author of this book, gives a somewhat different picture of Quantrill and the Lawrence raid than the usual one. Most people saw the Lawrence raid as an example of Quantrill's complete lack of human decency. They thought he had ordered his men to kill as many people as possible—men, women, and children—and to utterly destroy the town. Goodrich shows that this was not what really happened, and that Quantrill was probably not the "devil" many people thought he was.

We may never get a truly balanced picture of the Civil War and the people who fought in it, but if people like Tom Goodrich keep looking back at that time and trying to understand what really happened, we should get a clearer picture of what was one of the most difficult times in our country's history.

For More Reading

The American Heritage Picture History of the Civil War, by Bruce Catton (New York: American Heritage/Bonanza Books, 1960), provides a good general overview of the Civil War with a large number of photographs, paintings, and maps.

Bloody Dawn: The Story of the Lawrence Massacre, by Thomas Goodrich (Kent, Ohio: Kent State University Press, 1991), offers a dramatic, well-written, and carefully researched account of this controversial 1863 raid into Kansas by one of the most important and most controversial Missouri guerrilla leaders.

Borderland Rebellion, by Elmo Ingenthron (Branson, Mo.: Ozarks Mountaineer Press, 1980), is one of the few books about the Civil War along the Missouri-Arkansas border by a well-known Ozark educator and historian who makes good use of many eyewitness accounts.

Civil War on the Western Border, 1854–1865, by Jay Monaghan (Lincoln: University of Nebraska Press, 1955), a colorful history of the Civil War west of the Mississippi River, traces the development of the conflict in the West to the desperate struggle for "Bleeding Kansas" in the 1850s.

Damned Yankee: The Life of General Nathaniel Lyon, by Christopher Phillips (Columbia: University of Missouri Press, 1990), is the first full-length, modern biography of this important if short-lived Union general killed in the first year of the war in Missouri.

General Sterling Price and the Civil War in the West, by Albert Castel (Baton Rouge: Louisiana State University Press, 1968), is a good, modern study of Missouri's best-known Confederate general, focusing on all the major battles in which he took part.

Gray Ghosts of the Confederacy: Guerrilla Warfare in the West, 1861–1865, by Richard S. Brownlee (Baton Rouge: Louisiana State University Press, 1958), a former director of the State Historical Society of Missouri, is one of the best general studies of guerrilla warfare west of the Mississippi River.

In Deadly Earnest, by Phil Gottschalk (Columbia: Missouri River Press, 1991), is the story of the famous First Missouri Brigade that fought for the Confederacy throughout the war and includes many first-person accounts of battles, marches, and camp life.

Inside War: The Guerrilla Conflict in Missouri during the American Civil War, by Michael Fellman (New York: Oxford University Press, 1989), is perhaps the best book since Brownlee's classic study, mentioned above, on the subject of guerrilla warfare in Missouri, with a strong emphasis on firsthand accounts of the effects of this terrifying form of warfare on the civilian population of the state.

Jesse James Was His Name, by William A. Settle (Columbia: University of Missouri Press, 1966), provides the most balanced and trustworthy account of the career of this legendary Missouri outlaw.

Missouri Sketchbook, by Clifton C. Edom (Columbia, Mo.: Lucas Brothers Publishing, 1962), gives an excellent collection of illustrations relating to the Civil War in Missouri compiled by a veteran teacher of photojournalism at the University of Missouri's School of Journalism.

Noted Guerrillas, or the Warfare of the Border, by John Newman Edwards (Dayton, Ohio: Morningside Bookshop Reprint, 1976), is the classic early account and defense of guerrilla

warfare in Missouri, originally published in 1877, by a jour-
nalist who rode with Missouri Confederate General Jo Shelby
during the war, knew the guerrillas personally, and became
their chief apologist in the years following the war.

Pea Ridge: Civil War Campaign in the West, by William L. Shea
and Earl J. Hess (Chapel Hill: University of North Carolina
Press, 1992), offers a detailed, well-researched, and dramatic
account of this significant battle along the Missouri-Arkansas
border in 1862.

Quantrill and the Border Wars, by William E. Connelley (Ot-
tawa, Kans.: Kansas Heritage Press, 1992), is a reprint of the
classic, though one-sided, 1910 study of the most notorious
Civil War guerrilla leader in Missouri by the longtime sec-
retary of the Kansas State Historical Society.

Shelby and His Men, by John Newman Edwards (Waverly, Mo.:
General Joseph Shelby Memorial Fund, 1993), reprints another classic originally published in 1867, giving a colorful,
though obviously prejudiced, account of the career of this
dashing Missouri Confederate cavalry leader.

Songs of the Civil War, edited by Irwin Silber (New York:
Bonanza Books, 1960), is one of the best and most complete
collections of Civil War songs (both words and music) with
detailed notes about the backgrounds of the songs.

William Clarke Quantrill, His Life and Times, by Albert Castel
(Columbus, Ohio: General's Books, 1992), is a reprint of
the best and most objective modern account of the career
of this famous Missouri guerrilla leader, originally published
in 1962.

A FINAL NOTE

There are, of course, many more books on the subject of the
Civil War, though the ones listed here are the main ones
relating to the Civil War west of the Mississippi River.

Many TV documentaries have been made in recent years
about the Civil War, but one of the best of these is the fine
series made for PBS by Ken Burns.

There are also numerous recordings of Civil War music that the reader is encouraged to listen to as a way of getting a better feel for the subject and the times. The author of this book, along with well-known midwestern folksingers Cathy Barton and Dave Para, in the spring of 1993 recorded the only known collection of Civil War songs specifically related to the Civil War in Missouri, Kansas, and Arkansas. This collection, which is available on both cassette tape and compact disc from Big Canoe Records, 513 High Street, Boonville, Missouri, 65233, is called *Johnny Whistletrigger: Civil War Songs from the Western Border.*

Your library can help you find these books and other materials on the Civil War.

Index

Abolitionists, 9

American Weekly, 68

Anderson, William C. ("Bloody Bill"): origin of nickname, 33; physical description of, 33; early years in Huntsville, Missouri, and Kansas, 33; forms guerrilla band, 33; sister killed in Kansas City building collapse, 33; photo of, 34; Frank James joins, 39; Jesse James joins, 39–42; incident in Rocheport, Missouri, 42; raid on Fayette, Missouri, 42; Centralia Massacre, 42; meets Gen. Sterling Price in Boonville, 42–43, 45; killed in Ray County, Missouri, 43, 48, 49 (photo of in death); James gang avenges killing of, 52–53

Anti-slavery movement, 9, 11–12, 14

Appomattox Courthouse, 48

Bates County, Missouri, 37

Battles: of Carthage, 22; of Fort Davidson (Pilot Knob), 44, 45 (illustration of); of Lexington (Hemp Bales), 27–28 (with illustration); of Pea Ridge, 30–31 (with illustration), 74 (photo of monument on battlefield); of Westport, 47–48; of Wilson's Creek, 22–26 (with illustration), 32

Baxter Springs, Kansas, 39

Big Blue River. *See* Battles: of Westport

Bingham, George Caleb, 38

Blair, Francis, 19–20

"Bloody Hill," 25. *See also* Battles: of Wilson's Creek

Blue Cut, Missouri, 61

Blue Springs, Missouri, 14

Blunt, General James G., 39

Books about Jesse James: *I Jesse James*, 70; *Jesse James Was His Name*, 69; *Jesse James Was My Neighbor*, 69; *The Life, Times and Treacherous Death of Jesse James*, 69; *The Rise and Fall of Jesse James*, 69. *See also* Movies about Jesse James; Plays about Jesse James

Boonville, Missouri, 19, 21 (illustration of Battle of), 42, 45, 73

Booth, John Wilkes, 48

About the Author

Robert L. Dyer. (Bob Barrett photo)

Robert L. Dyer is a filmmaker, historian, folklorist, poet, and former English teacher who lives in Boonville, Missouri. He has published a book of poetry (*Oracle of the Turtle*), a history of his hometown (*Boonville: An Illustrated History*), and a collection of his own songs based on Missouri history and folklore (*Big Canoe Songbook*). He was writer and codirector of a film about the American epic poet John Neihardt titled *Performing the Vision*. He has made two recordings of his original folk-style ballads (*River of the Big Canoes* and *Treasure in the River*), and he provided the music for the University of Missouri film *Tom Benton's Missouri*, about Benton's Missouri State Capitol mural. For the past ten years he has been an active participant in the Missouri Arts Council's Artist-in-Education program and in the Arts Partners program sponsored by Young Audiences of Kansas City, Inc.